Heartbeats

Matthew Scholes

BookLeaf Publishing

Presentation by *BookLeaf Publishing*

Web: www.bookleafpub.com

E-mail: info@bookleafpub.com

ISBN: 9789357691581

First edition 2022

DEDICATION

To my long suffering, wonderful wife Charlotte, who has had to put up with me talking about writing (and apparently not doing much of it) for many years.

For Archie and Eleanor. One day, all will become clear.

'Those who think on things of earth are slowly dying; yet those who dream do not fear death.' (Author)

ACKNOWLEDGEMENT

This book would not have been possible without the people that inspired it: Some are loves remembered, others were friends and some of them still are. A successful life is built with these friendships and relationships, and we are less successful and less happy without them. It is the actions and words of others that serve to inspire us all.

I am most grateful to God, whom I believe has guided me to the place I am today, as he can guide all of us.

PREFACE

In the fifteen years or so that the majority of
these works were penned, we've seen how the
internet has taken over the world and how
phones have become computers. One of the
interesting themes that a reader might find here,
is the sense of change and of adaptation, both to
technology and also to growing up. And, partly
because I was a teenager and then student when
I wrote many of them, the rules are consciously
broken; the rules of grammar, spelling and
punctuation are experimented with. I hope the
effect is an interesting one.

Enjoy. Let the words take you. I don't expect
you to like every poem – that is never the case
with any poetry collection – but I'd love to know
which ones you do respond well to, and which
resonate positively with you.

'Tis with our judgements, as our watches. None
go just alike, yet each believes his own.'
(Alexander Pope, An Essay on Criticism)

Time

Time flashes on
quicker than light itself,
it flies, breaks free – unstoppable,
it is our fiercest enemy.

Time takes away
your freedom, eats away your youth
and prevents you from remembering
what made you; your essence.
Your truth.

REDISCOVER
Before it's too late.

Shallow Breaths

He sits there, eyes staring
concentrating on nothing.
The brow creased,
shoulders tense,
shallow breaths;
painfully,
permanently silent.

I wonder what troubles him?
The unshaking head must ache,
all that pent up hate,
the anger
clear for all to see
tight and un-listening
he seems
almost dead to me.

Perhaps he has suffered
some great loss –
a cherished one,
a great friend,
a love gained then lost,
or perhaps he is overflowing
with regret,
totally consumed by fear.

I turn away from the mirror in plain disgust and
ask myself….
What is it that hurts me?

Skit

For what are we?
When all said and done,
but a heap of bones and blood,
with a brain that screws us up.
And stupid thoughts that cause more harm than good.
I can't know the future. I can't see my way ahead.
All I can do is trust that He does, put aside my pride
and have the humility to be led.

He who thinks on things of earth is slowly dying, but
he who dreams does not fear death.

Game of hearts

You scroll up the menu
Select
Begin the game

You concentrate
Then select three cards to pass
And make your first mistake

You play the same players
Try and test – experiment
Search for a pattern

Eventually – you win a game
Some accomplishment
Another feeling is just the same

I look at the picture of her
Inside my wallet
And remember – it's the same thing
Addiction – a game, a person
That's the way it starts…

You know that
eventually, you'll win,
but first you'll lose – a lot.

That's just the way it is
when you play the game of hearts.

Peace

There's an image in my mind
that makes me smile
Golden trees in a stately line
a bubbling, dashing stream
calm greenery
A peaceful scene, locked in time

Nobody can destroy the image
Dare I challenge the devil himself?
Your mind cannot envisage victory
mine misgives, values its own health
but what gifts are given me
that I cannot return...?

Wise men and women are not always right
They simply learn.

HEALER

Moments, frozen
by virtue of their place in time
can and will return to haunt you
if by others they are chosen
and used as sharpened axes...
to cut away the shreds
of your credibility.

Sometimes all that
you are, all you have achieved
becomes naught, when one
such moment causes
your embarrassment...
and the laughs of those you loved
are caught,
echoing in your mind.

All your work undone,
all your sacrifices rent
in broken dreams and burning,
smoulder at your feet.

Sharp silence.
Inner pain to take away your hope.

So,   how will you recover
and what can you do to heal?
Time will ease the worst of it,
new places, new dreams
can replace the old...
forgetfulness and forgiveness
will be your closest friends.

Rhythm of the heart

Heart, stretched thin
moulded, softly
with eyes of glass and legs of tin
it beats its steady time…

as the fleshy sides keep pumping,
the body struggles, hurts,
but still standing – fights – and keeps this
simple, sinful mind
continually, inevitably working.

The Charge (inspired by Rohan's riders in The Return of the King)

The wind tugs at the eaves of this stately home.
I occupy a room of dreams,
with its high ceiling and rich tapestry.
Having seen the battle and wanted to be in it
myself,
inside lies a deeper sense of history.

I ride forward alongside my brothers into battle,
we carry the standard of our King.
We are knights – glorious in our army – we fly,
like this howling wind. Our swords flash,
the hooves of our horses sing.

There before us lies the enemy.
His fiercest troops face us – their snarling faces
grimace;
even the bravest feels fear.
But the warmth of our spirit drives us on.
Caught up in a seething, relentless mass of
helmets, hooves and shields,
we are no longer individuals – we are one.

There is one purpose only. To win the fight. And
one choice to be made – to live or die.

Surely this is what we have dreamt of?
A great sense of happiness and hope fills my
soul,
even with the sharpest steel and strongest cries
of our deadly foe,
ringing in my ears.
I channel it, it does not dull my wits – but makes
me stronger – one moment.
One moment
to banish all our fear.

Christmas

There is an end of things, but first there was a
beginning;
memories of snow packed in woollen gloves and
gangs of children singing.
A Christmas tree with brilliant lights, a cold
wind, wet and stinging.
the end of one year and the breaking of the next,
but first
before the end of things, there is always a
beginning.

There was a manger with straw, dirt, the stink of
animals,
a windowless shack, dimly lit, its timbers gently
creaking.
Inside, a tiny baby wrapped in swaddling cloths,
his deep eyes stare past the walls
His mother lifts her head and offers a quiet
prayer of thanksgiving.
Meanwhile, in the distant heavens, throngs of
angels are joyfully singing.

There is an end of things, but first there is a
beginning;

a sin filled earth, death, pain, emptiness,
loneliness, all kinds of suffering…
broken hearts, brittle promises, revenge,
jealousy, anger, this devil has so many guises!
And yet. There is hope. Remember, if we despair
then he will win.
There is an end of things, but first there was a
beginning.

Answers

My ear cracks for the tenth rhyme as I stare back in time
I'm looking through a mirror, past the purple journal
I can see where we have gone wrong. Dare to be a Daniel.
Who are you? Are you really willing, to reveal all and tell
us your darkest secrets? No. Fear stops your mouth and
Darkness covers your brightest light.

Maybe my head is overheating and still frightened,
I could tell you more than I have. What prevents us? In the
end.
It's the soft wood that rests my arms. That's what keeps
us from finding truth. The plastic that covers my computer.
The metal that covers this lamp. Safety. Security. Nothing
will ever stop you going crazy.

Distraction. That's the enemy's trump card. Illusion. Not
AI. DI, all to die, that's what one side of the war wants.
Funny thing is, some of you already know that lying
may be by far the better option. Not knowing, not caring.
Who
were you before you existed? Good people will ask
impossible-to-answer questions.

That's the hard part of being of human. Sitting here
with my aching limbs and poppy ear, cauliflower nose
and shiny glass tears. I'm doing it too. Spots and smelly
privates. Itchy scratches. Things people don't like to say
but that doesn't make them go away. Irony. God's
sense of humour. Hilarious.

What gives him the right to watch me struggle? Maybe
I haven't understood. It's not for want of trying. Don't

you want to understand why you're here? Oh. You're
one of them… the ones who think this is it. Don't make
me laugh. If all I have and all I am is here and now
then I am nothing to too many people.

So that's why I have to believe. That's why I want to
Understand. Meaning. Knowing what happens when I
Tap these keys. Tap, tap, over and over again, even more
When I make a mistake (which I often do). The chain.
The reaction. How does it work? Don't we have a right to
know? I'm tired of asking questions.
We need answers. We've all got questions.
That's why we have wars, and revolutions.
Ask one too many and 'BANG!'
Go on, smile.

Gunshot

Assume the position. No giggling ladies. Now, make the weapon ready. Click, smoosh, clack, kuchunk. Load the weapon. Click, clonk.   Cock the weapon. Kochonk. Look down the sight to the centre of the target. You have the order to fire. Take a deep breath. Breathe out and relax. At the end of the breath, with the sight resting above the centre spot – pull the

>>

    trigger, gently and let   h   go, slowly > > > >
     BANG!! But you only   a   hear
    a muffled thud – you   p py   are
    wearing ear plugs. t r i g g e r
  There is a slight kick
  the shoulder resists
 nothing to worry
 about. Just another
 shot. One more on
 the dot. Plum centre
  So that's it then. ALL
  There is to it. Not really.
 Can you do it when it counts?

Grand Ideas 2

Fight with purpose and you will grow in love.
Passion burns, it is not a vapour or a flower,
for it can never be weakness,
but can only be pure, sterile strength.
And then, when it is for the good,
it can achieve infinitely more than
a mighty army of thousands ever could.

Climb

We four specs of dust
clamber up this monster
with its hard face and grey wrinkles stretching
out
along the valley's base
through river, through trees, across heather
covered ground.
The mountain isn't fussed
it is oblivious, it doesn't care
But we ache and tire and scramble
hoping that Matt's knee will handle it, that
David and Kevin won't fade
between rocks, over streams, around imposing
bluffs.

More than a morning amble
we fight against the angles
struggle, but succeed, and find a stiff
north-easterly breeze
flying around the top, shouting and moaning
wishing that we hadn't made it. But we did.

Coming down
no time for clowning around
on slippery rocks and into biting blizzard

Andy obliviously walks on, with his powerful experience
driving him. While we carry our battered limbs
across the last mile. And grimace with victory.

SHAKEN Written in Sri Lanka in 2005, just a few months after the Boxing Day Tsunami devastated the East coast, where the author visited.

Bedraggled, stinking, greenery
droops, drapes across this face;
unwillingly, she parts the strands
and peers through - the light breaks
on a different view, a new land...

Milk and honey flow, but where do
these rivers go? To the sea or to the
hills? This land is upside down,
the wrong way round; water flows uphill
and the mountains are underground.

Secret Smile

The image of that secret smile that my memory holds
Has waxed and waned as I've grown old
And though I still can hear the sounds and see the sights
They are blurred and faint, for I have new memories
And new dreams; it just seems right that
When I meet you I should know where we last met
And how long ago
It's just polite
To ask 'How are you?'
And then the image of your face is engraved on my mind
And each new engraving distorts the older ones
Like, at night, when you close your eyes and
pictures flash in front of you like slides
I just know that at some point, I'll see your face, your eyes
And remember the old engraving
The faded painting
Of your secret smile.

Railway Journey

Like a single, bright light in the darkness
We time travel to a time when iron, horse and stone
Rule the world.
Now we are free. I live your kindness and you are
Almost all of me
The moment is meaningless, nowhere is our
Greatest goal – we are supernatural and
As children we sparkle and glow
We have turned and spoken across the aisle between us
Time travelled to a time when iron, horse and stone
Ruled the world.

We can grasp the solid truth of what has been
Feel certain in the promises of the constant hum
Of forever-turning wheels
Furiously traversing earth.
You are perfectly pure, clean of sin – and you
And I travel through time,
The chords and chimes of fascination
Tied between us
To a time when iron, horse, and stone ruled the world
Finding, to our surprise,
that we are King & Queen of all.

an i ma ge

Sometimes all you need to inspire you is an
image. Say:
A girl
walking through an English wood
in autumn
with the orange-yellow leaves strewn around
on the ground
and odd red ones
floating gently to their hallowed graves.
A wet, damp place.
The pale sun filters through the web-like
branches
casting long shadows
where the air is cooler.
It is very still.

Can you feel it? Are you there with her?

Say:
A man walking through a crowded English city,
his briefcase held against his leg
his smart, grey suit
with the red metallic tie
his glasses
with the gold trim

a sharp ring to his shoes as they strike
the concrete pathways of the metropolis.
The buildings tower over him and shoppers,
businessmen, tourists, children,
the lost, the hungry,
all with their destinations
(none going anywhere)
walk and run…

Can you see his face? Where is he going?

Remember your image. The image of yourself:
Can you feel it?
Is it really you?
Where are you going?

Reopstia

I went out today.
Tipped a wink.
Bought a book.
Shot a snake.
And washed the blood out in a white, ceramic
sink.

I went wandering today. In my head.
Killed an enemy.
Ran away.
My friend was murdered. He's dead.
I went shopping today.
No I didn't.

I went out today.
Tipped a wink.
Made love.
Got famous:
Yeah, right.

I went wandering today.
Outside my head.
Did nothing.
Still dead.

I remembered today.
I thought about someone else.
Alive.
Resurrected.

I stayed in today.
Tomorrow I'm going to save the world.

Yeah, that's right.

Shining metal

As I gaze upon this sea
of shining metal, white and flat
My memories come back to me.
Each pane of glass is set in brick
each blade of grass stands, proud and thick
casting their shadows and their raise
upon my eyes, as I gaze.

As I look and drink and see
I cannot help but think of me –
me as a writer, tip, tap, tip,
them as a pin, thin, but quick.
The sun slants off these thoughts
and soon, I will commence the idiom
seen, purple, reflected in my spoon.

Reflections are but images – not real
but flying over heads of thought
and recalling those old memories (not sold to
friends, but bought).
The shadows of the trees move jerkily
and men clutch at their hats
and women at their skirts.
This, is what I see
when I gaze, longingly
at air and space and shining metal.

the picture (a teenager's poem)

i see her when i feel the sun on my face.
It reminds me of the time i saw her
leaning against the cottage wall
whitewashed cottages look beautiful;
this one looked better with her beneath it.
Innocent and alone she read her book
under the warm, Welsh sun
with its rays shining from her face.
Have you ever seen an Angel?

i see her when i sit alone in my room
And think of all the miles between us –
wondering
If she has forgotten the day i gave her wild
flowers.
i sometimes feel (when i write about someone)
That i have betrayed their trust
That things between that person and myself
Become more complicated.

I hope not.
I will remember my simple picture
And trust that she will remember hers.

Ode to Nevis

These majestic mounds
elevated
hill upon hill
so high
as the air thins
it becomes pure
washed
like linen
and bleached by sky

Peace that time cannot weaken.
Peace that tastes like freedom.
Peace that smooths away
your face's pain.
A spiritual calm,
made perfect
by the passing rain.

These towering mountains
do not change with time
they have drawn
unalterable lines
their spirit
freedom
remains the same

paths weathered
trampled
and yet unchanged.

It's 10:31 Somewhere

Karen Conway